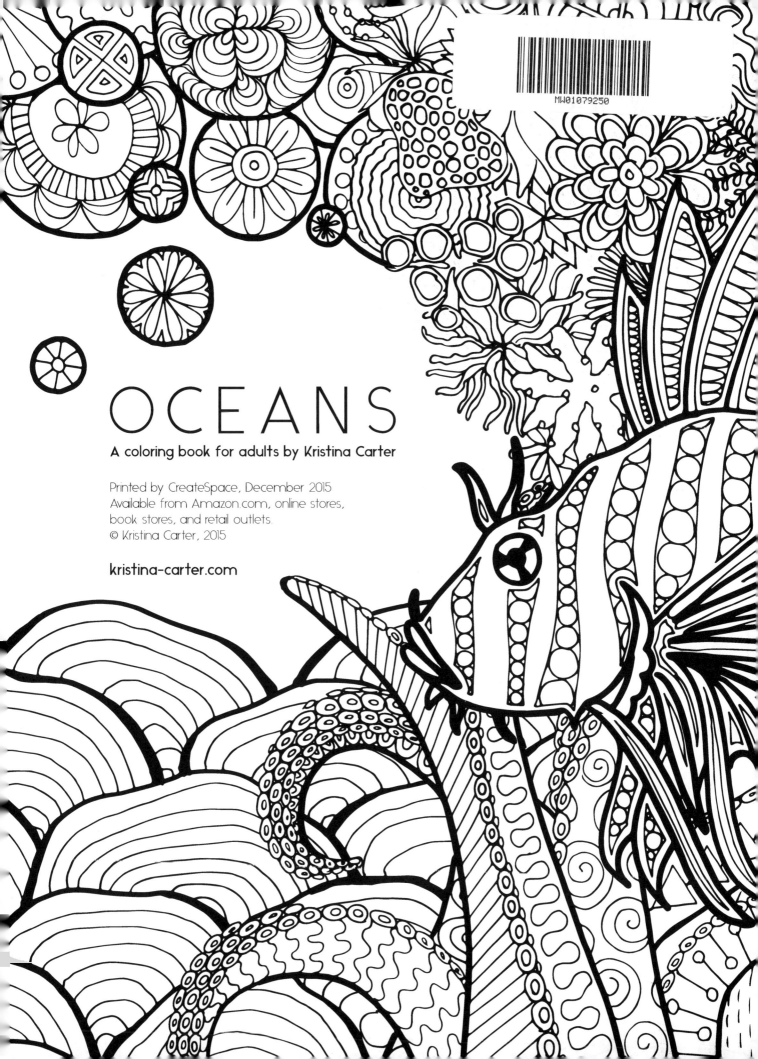

OCEANS

A coloring book for adults by Kristina Carter

Printed by CreateSpace, December 2015
Available from Amazon.com, online stores,
book stores, and retail outlets.
© Kristina Carter, 2015

kristina-carter.com

This book belongs to:

_____

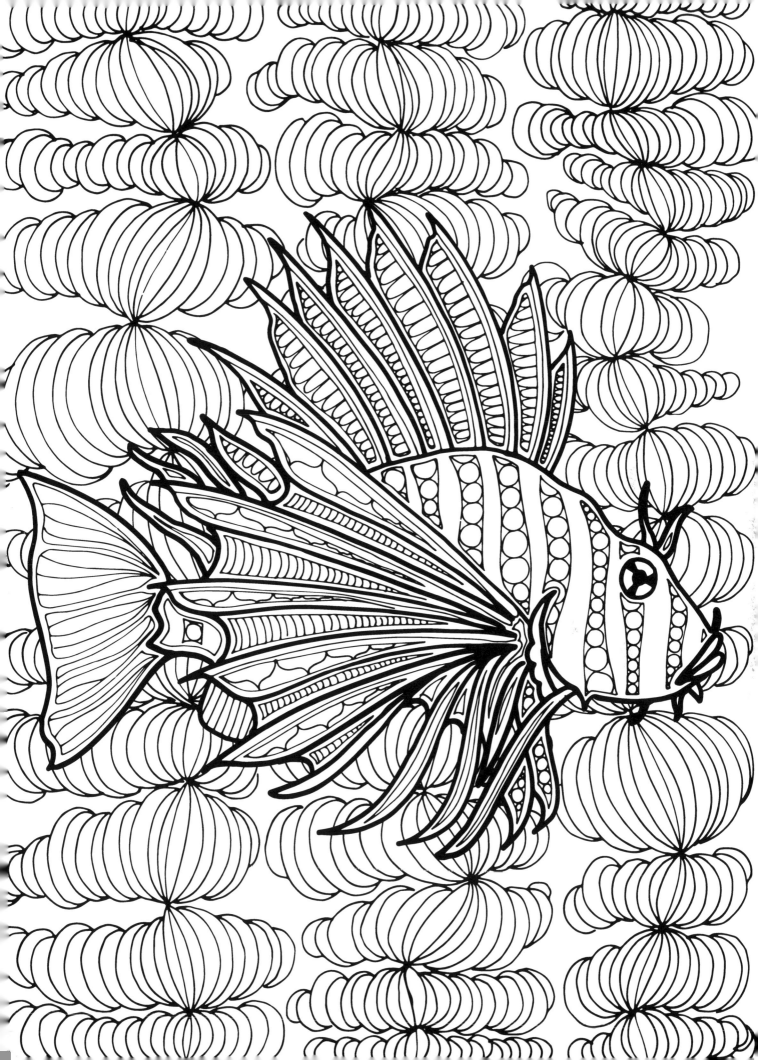

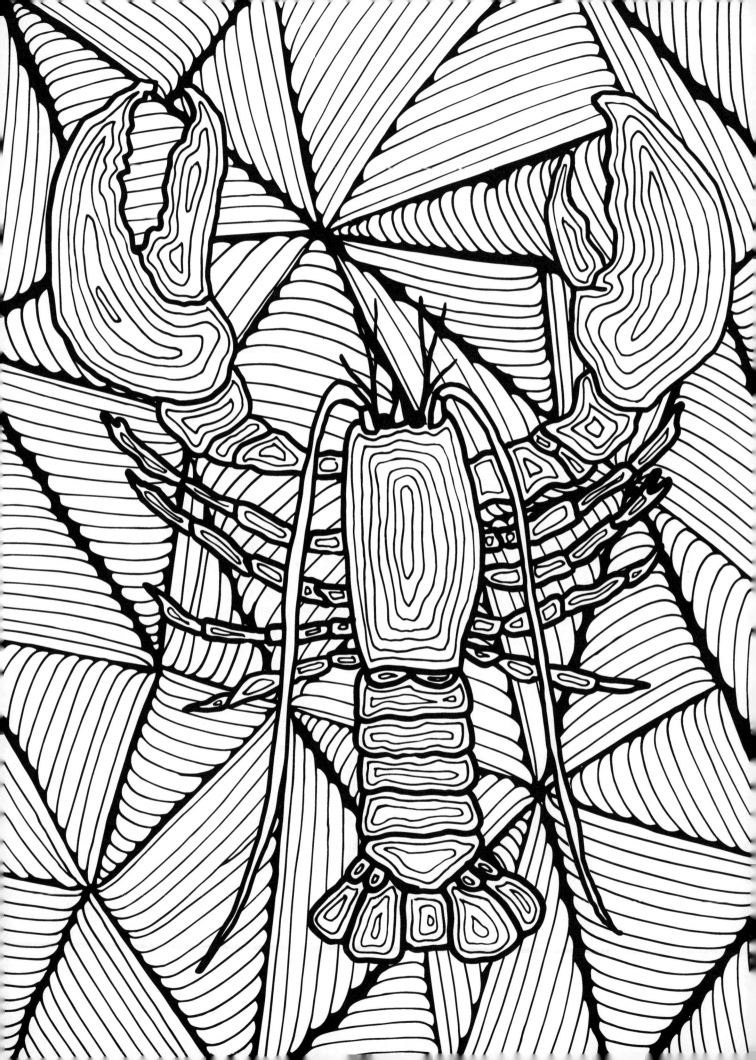

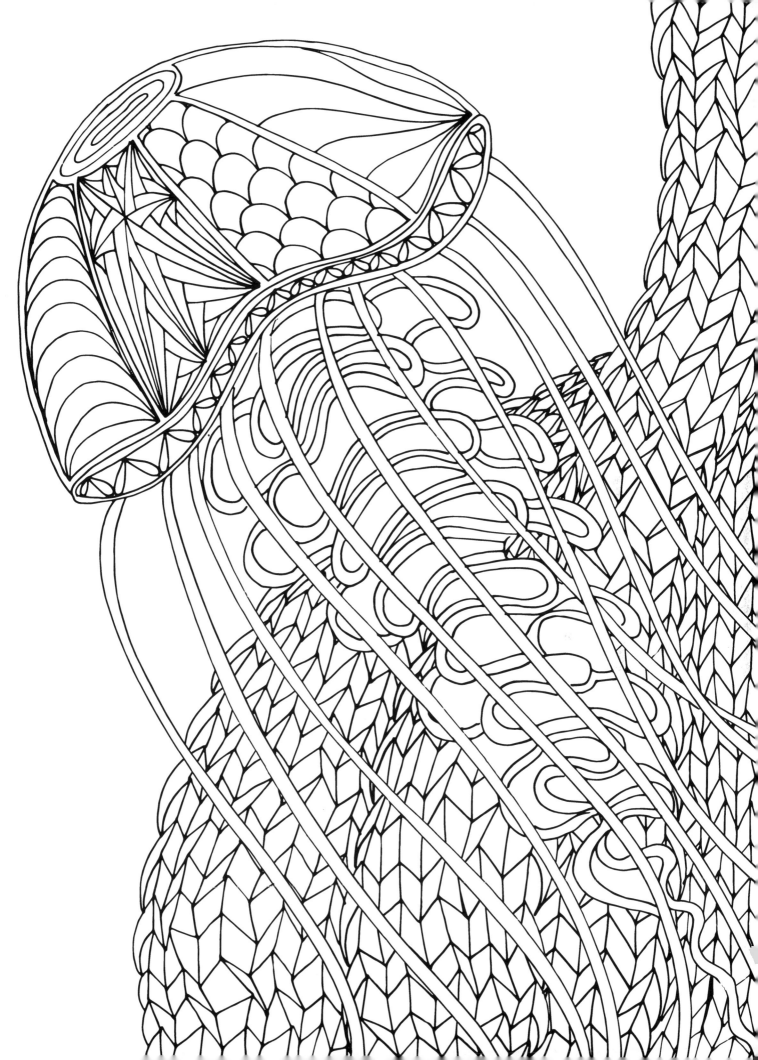

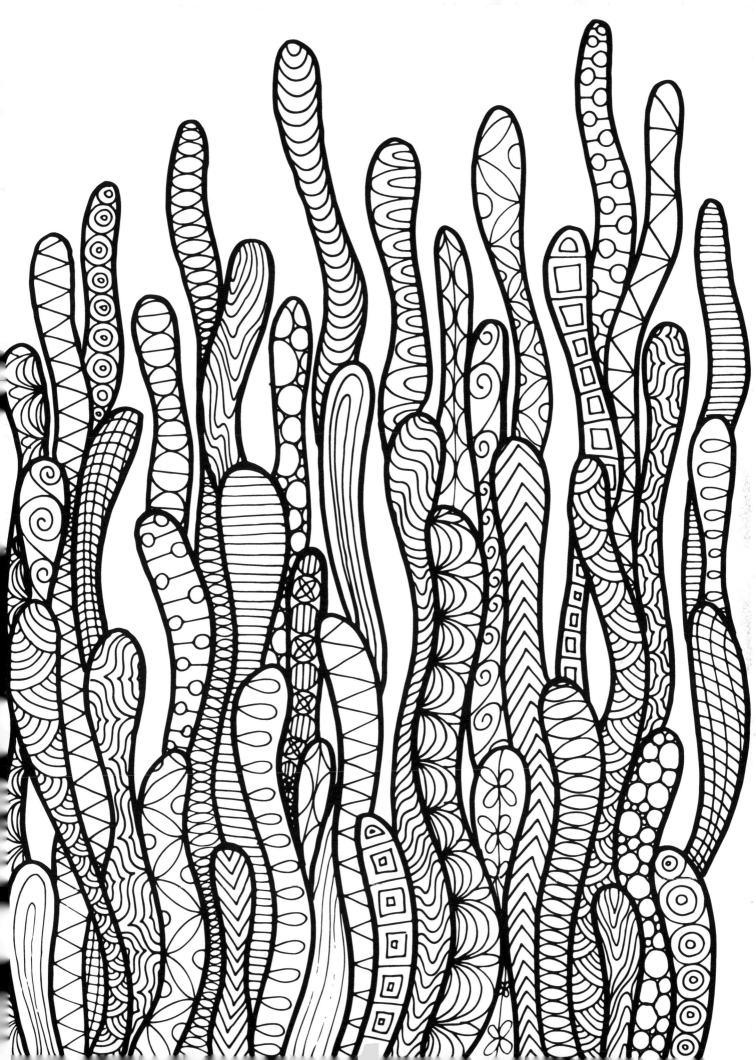

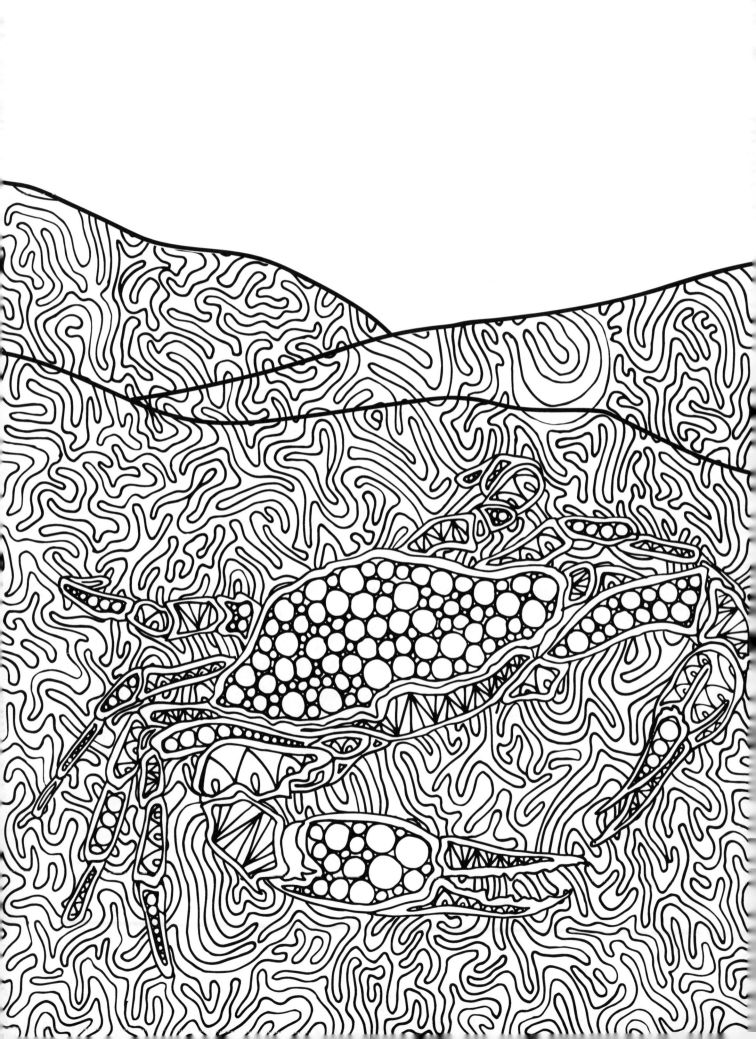

Made in the USA
San Bernardino, CA
02 June 2016